INFORMATION
EXPLORER
JUNIOR

Getting
Around Online

by Kristin Fontichiaro

CHERRY LAKE PUBLISHING · ANN ARBOR, MICHIGAN

CHERRY LAKE
Publishing

A NOTE TO PARENTS AND TEACHERS:
Please remind your children how to stay safe online before they do the activities in this book.

A NOTE TO KIDS:
Always remember your safety comes first!

Published in the United States of America
by Cherry Lake Publishing
Ann Arbor, Michigan
www.cherrylakepublishing.com

Content Adviser: Gail Dickinson, PhD, Associate Professor, Old Dominion University

Book design and illustration: The Design Lab

Photo credits: Cover, ©iStockphoto.com/video1; page 6, ©Ricardo Alday/Shutterstock, Inc.; pages 9 and 18, ©Dmitriy Shironosov/Shutterstock, Inc.; page 12, ©Annette Shaff/Shutterstock.com.

Library of Congress Cataloging-in-Publication Data

Fontichiaro, Kristin.
  Getting around online / by Kristin Fontichiaro.
    p. cm.—(Information explorer junior)
  Includes bibliographical references and index.
  ISBN 978-1-61080-366-3 (lib. bdg.)—ISBN 978-1-61080-375-5 (e-book)—
ISBN 978-1-61080-391-5 (pbk.)
1. Internet searching—Juvenile literature. I. Title.
  ZA4230F66 2012
  025.042'5—dc23   2011037592

Cherry Lake Publishing would like to acknowledge
the work of The Partnership for 21st Century Skills.
Please visit *www.21stcenturyskills.org* for more information.

Printed in the United States of America
Corporate Graphics Inc.
January 2012
CLSP10

Table of Contents

CHAPTER ONE

Searching for Answers

Suppose you and a few friends are playing a game of soccer. It starts out friendly until after one of the plays. Suddenly, everyone begins to argue about the rules. You agree to keep playing. But when you get home, you wonder what the correct rule is. How do you find out?

Follow the rules to keep games fun and fair.

The Internet has information about almost any subject you can think of.

One great place to find information is on the **Internet**. The Internet is an electronic **network**. Computers around the world are connected together. Words, videos, pictures, sounds, conversations, and e-mails are found on billions of pages. All of them make up the Internet.

Each browser looks a little different, but any of them can help you find the information you need.

You get onto the Internet using the **browser** in your computer. A browser is a computer program. It allows you to look through pages and other information that appears on the Internet. Popular browsers are Internet Explorer, Safari, Firefox, and Chrome.

Once you are online, you can use a **search engine**. It looks for the words or information you request. Some good search engines for kids are:

- *kids.yahoo.com*
- *www.kidsclick.org*
- *www.askkids.com*

Activity

Open a browser on a computer at home or at school. If you need help, ask your teacher or librarian. Type in the words *soccer rules*. Then press Return or Enter on your keyboard.

How many results did you get? What kind of information about soccer rules did you find?

To get a copy of this activity, visit www.cherrylakepublishing.com/activities.

CHAPTER TWO

Keywords

Your search for *soccer rules* probably produced thousands of Web pages. Maybe even millions of pages! What if you spent just one second looking at each page? It would take you months to see them all. Wow!

Strategies help you find what you need fast!

Choosing good keywords makes it easy to find the information you are looking for.

There are so many choices. How do you find the information you need? With **strategies**! A strategy is a tool or clever plan that helps you reach your goal.

When we look for information online, we are searching. Smart searchers think about the words that describe what they are looking for. We call these words **keywords**. Usually, they are nouns. Nouns are the names of people, places, or things.

The size of a baseball is just one of the many facts you are sure to find online.

Let's say you want to find out the size of a baseball. Your question is, "How big is a baseball?" There are two main ideas in that question. One is size. *Big* is an **adjective**. For your search, use the noun *size*. The other idea is baseball. Go to your search engine's search box. Type in *size baseball*.

Or maybe your question is, "What kind of pet is best for my family?" Great keywords are *family pet*, *household pet*, and *safe pet*.

Skip short, common words in your search. You don't need to type in *is*, *the*, *a*, *for*, *of*, or *my*. You can also skip capital letters and punctuation. But spell carefully. A friend or grown-up can help.

Activity

Practice turning these questions into keywords:

- When is the next full moon?
- How old is Barack Obama?
- How do you play basketball?
- What is the distance from New York City, New York, to Los Angeles, California?

1. Open a blank page in your notebook. Use a ruler to draw a line down the center of the page. You should now have two long boxes.

2. Write "Question" at the top of the box on the left. Write the four questions from the list above in this box.

3. Write "Keywords" at the top of the box on the right. Write the names of the keywords you would use to search for answers to the questions.

To get a copy of this activity, visit www.cherrylakepublishing.com/activities.

11

CHAPTER THREE

Understanding Results

It only takes a second to get the results of a search. A list of Web pages will appear on your computer screen. Each item in the list is called a **hit**.

Google is the most popular search engine.

Hyperlink →

Soccer Rules-Rules Of Soccer

Learn how to play soccer using American rules. ←

Snippet

Remember your search for *soccer rules*? Let's go back and look at the results.

Some words are underlined in blue. These underlined words are called **hyperlinks**, or links. Click on the link. You will be taken to that Web page.

Below each hyperlink are a few words called a **snippet**. A snippet briefly tells you what is on that page. Read the snippets to see if a page seems useful and easy to read. Many Web sites were made for adults. These snippets might be hard to read. If so, click on another result.

Are you using Google or Bing as your search engine? Images or videos about your subject might come up. Do your search. Then click on "Image" or "Video" in the left column.

Google guesses which Web sites will help you most. It lists those sites at the top of your results. Some hits may not be helpful. That's because a machine made the list for you. A person might have made a different list.

Keep a list of the Web sites you use for a project. It's how you show where you found the information. You'll be able to find it again, too! Write the Web site's address (such as *www.whitehouse.gov*). Don't write the address of the search engine.

Activity

Look through your search results for *soccer rules*.

- Which three sites look the most helpful? Why?
- Which three look the least helpful? Why?

To get a copy of this activity, visit www.cherrylakepublishing.com/activities.

1. Take two sheets of paper from your notebook.
2. On the first sheet, use a ruler to draw a line down the center of the page. You should now have two long boxes. Write "Most Helpful" at the top of the column on the left. Write "Reasons Why" at the top of the column on the right.
3. On the second sheet, draw a line down the center of the page. Write "Least Helpful" at the top of the column on the left. Write "Reasons Why" at the top of the column on the right.
4. Now write your answers to the questions.

Most Helpful	Reasons Why		Least Helpful	Reasons Why

CHAPTER FOUR

Narrowing Your Search

Roberto loves football, especially the Buffalo Bills. He wants to learn more about his favorite team. He types in the keywords *buffalo* and *bills*. Some results are about the football team. But some are about animals called buffalo! Or about a man named Buffalo Bill! Or about a buffalo nickel!

How can Roberto just get results about the football team? He needs to narrow his search. That way, he will get fewer hits. Roberto can add quotation marks around the words "buffalo bills." This tells the search engine to list certain Web pages. Those pages have the word *buffalo* next to the word *bills*. Web sites

16

about buffalo nickels won't show up. Buffalo Bill the man won't, either. Why? Because the search is for *bills*, not *bill*.

Activity

If you search for *"george washington,"* which of these snippets might show up?

a. George Washington was the first president of the United States.

b. George visited Washington, D.C., this summer.

c. George Smith and Mary Washington were married.

d. Our neighbor, Mrs. George, moved to Seattle, Washington.

Did you guess "a"? You're right! The other results don't have *george* and *washington* right next to each other.

To get a copy of this activity, visit www.cherrylakepublishing.com/activities.

CHAPTER FIVE

Subject Directories

Most libraries offer useful subject directories that you can use for free.

A **subject directory** is another good tool. It can help you find information on the Internet. Subject directories are collections of

Web sites gathered and organized by people. They start with a few main categories. Then they branch out into **subtopics**.

Suppose you wanted to find information about black bear cubs. Go to a subject directory. Start by clicking on *mammals*. Then click on *bears*. Then try *black bears*. You narrow your subject each time you click on a subtopic. This strategy is called drilling down.

What if you drill down and don't find any information? Back up! Try another path. Most subject directories also have a search box.

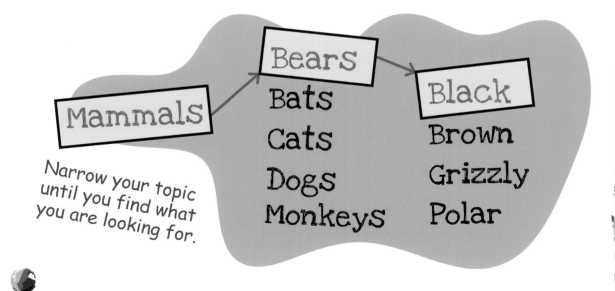

Mammals → Bears → Black

Bats
Cats
Dogs
Monkeys

Brown
Grizzly
Polar

Narrow your topic until you find what you are looking for.

Activity

Ask your teacher or librarian to show you one of these subject directories:

1. KidSpace at the Internet Public Library (*www.ipl.org/div/kidspace*)
2. National Geographic Kids (*http://kids.nationalgeographic.com/kids/animals/creaturefeature*)
3. SIRS Discoverer database (ask a librarian)
4. PebbleGo database (ask a librarian)

Do you like subject directories? Or do you like typing in keywords more? How are they different?

Here's a handy list to review what we've learned. It will help you get around online:

Review

- Type keywords, not an entire question or sentence.
- Turn adjectives such as *big* into nouns such as *size*.
- Leave out short words like *a*, *an*, *the*, and *of*.
- Don't worry about capital letters.
- Spelling counts!
- Use quotation marks to keep keywords together.
- Read over the snippets before you click. Look for helpful information that you can read.
- Click on "Image" or "Video" to see if there is more information you can learn.
- Keep a list of Web sites you visit (not the name of the search engine).
- Try a subject directory.

Follow these strategies to become an Internet super searcher!

Glossary

adjective (AJ-ik-tiv) a word that describes a noun or a pronoun

browser (BROW-zur) a computer program that lets you find and look through Web pages or other data

hit (HIT) a Web site that is displayed as the result of a search

hyperlinks (HYE-pur-links) references to Web pages that the reader can directly follow by clicking on them; also called links

Internet (IN-tur-net) the electronic network that allows millions of computers around the world to connect together

keywords (KEE-wurdz) words or phrases used to describe the contents of a document

network (NET-wurk) a system of things that are connected to each other

search engine (SURCH EN-juhn) a computer program that will help you find words or information you request

snippet (SNI-put) words that appear in search results that describe a Web site

strategies (STRA-tuh-jeez) tools or clever plans that help you reach your goal

subject directory (SUHB-jikt duh-REK-tuh-ree) a collection of Web sites gathered and organized by people, not computers

subtopics (SUB-ta-piks) more specific topics in a subject directory

Find Out More

BOOKS

Oxlade, Chris. *My First Internet Guide.* Chicago: Heinemann
    Library, 2007.

Rabbat, Suzy. *Super Smart Information Strategies: Find Your
    Way Online.* Ann Arbor, MI: Cherry Lake Publishing, 2010.

Truesdell, Ann. *Super Smart Information Strategies: Find the
    Right Site.* Ann Arbor, MI: Cherry Lake Publishing, 2010.

WEB SITES

Boolify

www.boolify.org

Check out this fun, interactive Web site to search the Internet.
You'll learn how to narrow your searches to get the best results.

KidsClick!

www.kidsclick.org/wows

You'll become a super Internet searcher using the tips and
strategies at this colorful, easy-to-follow site.

Index

About the Author

Kristin Fontichiaro teaches at the University of Michigan. She loves to learn new things online and spend time with her nieces and nephew. This is her third book for Cherry Lake Publishing.